3 3029 05503 5125

SACRAMENTO PUBLIC LIBRARY
828 "I" STREET
SACRAMENTO, CA 95814
10/2004

$\mathscr{B}$ABY $\mathscr{B}$UDDHAS

BABY BUDDHAS

A GUIDE FOR TEACHING MEDITATION TO CHILDREN

Lisa Desmond

Andrews McMeel Publishing

Kansas City

Baby Buddhas copyright © 2004 by Lisa Desmond. All rights reserved. Printed in Singapore. No part of this book may be used or reproduced in any manner whatsoever without written permission except in the case of reprints in the context of reviews. For information, write Andrews McMeel Publishing, an Andrews McMeel Universal company, 4520 Main Street, Kansas City, Missouri 64111.

04 05 06 07 08 TWP 10 9 8 7 6 5 4 3 2 1

Library of Congress Cataloging-in Publication Data

Desmond, Lisa.
   Baby buddhas : a guide for teaching meditation to children / Lisa Desmond.
     p. cm.
   ISBN 0-7407-4689-8
   1. Buddhist children—Religious life. 2. Meditation—Buddhism. I. Title: Guide for teaching meditation to children. II. Title.

BQ5436.D47 2004
204'.35'083—dc22

                                           2004047647

All photographs by Katrina Webster.
About the author photograph by Kimberly Ireland.

To the child within us all,
whose true home is in the place of love

Sophie—two years old

Contents

■

Adult Meditation for World Peace 49

*Gives adults a way to acknowledge and honor all adults and to
understand that all adults wish for the same thing—to raise all
children in a peaceful, loving world.*

Adult Meditation for Sending Love to a Child 57

*Gives adults who have in their lives a chronically ill child, a child
in a life-threatening situation, or a critically ill newborn a tool to
acknowledge and empower the bond of love.*

Part Three
Children's Meditations . . . 65

Sunshine Meditation 67

*Teaches children that love is within; builds self-esteem; helps with
depression.*

Contents

Teaches children that love is always with them; calms and comforts children; helps with separation anxiety; helps with hyperactivity.

Teaches children that they can let go of negative thoughts and feelings and replace them with positive ones; helps with tantrums; calms fears of new or frightening experiences; reduces anxiety; helps with hyperactivity.

Teaches children how to open up to the blessings within them and around them; helps with depression, apathy, and selfishness.

CONTENTS

■

CONTENTS

∎

Crystal Meditation 121

Teaches children that they are responsible for their actions, words, and thoughts; helps eliminate negative behavior such as hitting, biting, speaking unkindly, or running away from a parent; provides a tool that helps change behavior.

Rainbow Meditation 131

Teaches children that love heals and that love can be sent and received; helps with separation, illness, and death; provides a tool to use during difficult times.

In Closing 143

Acknowledgments

First of all, I would like to thank the monks and nuns of the Kopan Monestary, Kathmandu, Nepal. A special thank-you: To Namgyal, Gelick, and to the Hindu and Buddhist scholars and guides.

To Jim and Shelley Hagan of Wisdom Tours for sharing that part of the world with me.

To John and Mary Abele for their friendship and belief in me.

To Cheryl Storey for her unending dedication of time, wisdom, and seemingly never ending editing of this book.

To Fred and Ann Schmidt for planting the seed to write this book.

To my parents, Nils and Hellen Jonsson, who taught me the joy of being loved unconditionally.

To my sons, Joshua and Tyler who I love unconditionally, my first teachers.

To my grandparents Emma and Sune Franson, whose lives taught and emitted love, joy, and peace to me and all who knew them.

To my brothers and their families for their support and enthusiasm, Lance and Maryann Jonsson, Kerri, Talon, Kelly, Christy, and kind sweet Nick, Christopher and Wendy Jonsson, and adorable Casey and Lily.

∎

To my sister and her family for their encouragement and ideas, Linda and Don Ohlmeyer, Kemper, Drew, Wendy, and sweet Alexa and Skye, Chris, Julie, and cute Benjamin and Todd and Kati.

To Jackson Ohlmeyer who taught much in his short life and who inspired a meditation within this book.

To Tara Guber for her enthusiastic encouragement.

To Trina Webster for her incredible pictures.

To Chris, Suzanne, and George Davis for their support and beautiful space to teach in.

To my agent, Sabine Hrechdakin, who believed in this book from the beginning and helped me tremendously.

To Patty Rice and Andrews McMeel Publishing for their energy and enthusiasm.

To all the children and parents who have been in my program; without them this book would not be.

To Osel Dorje Rinpoche for his blessing of this book.

To my Guides, I am grateful for your patience, wisdom, joy, and love.

The spiral you see throughout this book
represents our inward journey to self-discovery
and our outward striving to unite all that is.

"Namaste"—Hadley, three years old

Introduction
The Beginning . . .

"Recently when asked, 'What does it feel like to meditate?'
Avery said, 'I open my heart and have loving feelings,'
all the while gesturing to her heart and mind."

— *Mother of two-year-old Avery*

The meditations in this book will give children a tool they can use in their daily lives, a tool that will last a lifetime. I have seen meditation work every day with the preschool children I teach. I have observed children who are in pain from the loss of a loved one, children who are sad, fearful, hyperactive, or angry, become calm, relaxed, and at peace with themselves and the world around them through meditation. It helps them to fall asleep and calms them when they are afraid, upset, or worried. It gives them a way to comfort themselves in times of grief and sorrow. It helps children with learning difficulties, attention deficits, and chronic or life-threatening illnesses build self-esteem and confidence through acceptance and understanding. I have seen the joy on a child's face when we do a meditation celebrating his or her birthday or the birthday of a sibling. I have seen relief on a child's face after he or she has sent love to a deceased relative or pet. Parents also see the benefits of meditation throughout the day. Children are "Ommming" themselves to sleep, sending love to friends and family whom they miss, and setting up a meditation space and meditating on their own, as they help themselves deal with fears like darkness and separation or celebrate a beautiful sunset or the arrival of a new brother or sister. Meditation gives children a way to send peace, joy, and love into a world they have yet to understand and gives them a way to take the time to be thankful and give gratitude for all they have, for the people who love them, and for the world they live in.

While I have found in my studies many styles of meditation interesting and enriching, the Tibetan Buddhist, Hindu, and Native American meditations are the ones that resonate with me most and are the ones that are reflected within this book. I had powerful and life-enhancing teachings from Tibetan monks at the Kopan Monastery in Nepal and Hindu and Tibetan Buddhist scholars and guides in Nepal and Tibet. While in Asia, I observed how spirituality was everywhere in these people's culture—in their architecture, their paintings and music, their speech, their every action and gesture. It became apparent to me that while Western cultures delved outside the self, Eastern cultures delved within. These trips reinforced my belief that children need to learn how to fill themselves and live their lives from the inside out. They can either spend their lives wondering who they are, searching outside of themselves for all the answers, or they can find a place of balance, harmony, and knowingness within. I have found that meditation provides a way and allows a child's true and authentic self to come forth and shine.

■

I had been teaching a traditional morning program in my home for children eighteen-months to three years old. As I became more interested in meditation, my home began to reflect my interests and the changes taking place within myself. I started playing calm, soothing, and healing music. I began collecting crystals, bells, chimes, singing bowls, Buddha statues, Indian rattles, and angels. I created altars for the sacred objects I brought home and with each new item the children's curiosity grew. They would ask: "Could I please hold that crystal?" "Who is that statue?" "Can you ring that bell?" "Can you show me how the singing bowl works?" "What's that angel's name?" "Could I shake that rattle?" I changed the popular kids'-style music I played to the more calming, soothing music I had begun listening to myself and saw, heard, and felt a real difference in the energy of the children. They were quieter and seemed more at peace. I began teaching the children about vibration—that the sound of "OM" is a vibration. That "OM" is in everything and everyone and that "OM" is the sound of love.

Their natural interest and curiosity made me wonder whether meditation could help children this young. The assumption is that preschoolers are not old enough to participate in such an adult activity, but research indicates that most of a child's learning takes place before the age of five. So, I began slowly piecing together, adapting, and creating meditations from what I was learning and practicing. I was open and sensitive to the children's own interests and needs, and together we created the different types and styles of meditations within this book.

Baby Buddhas has three parts. Part One, "Creating Your Space," teaches the fundamentals of meditating, such as breathing, posture, terminology, and how to create a successful environment for meditation. It is a guide to help all adults learn meditation and how to teach meditation to children. Part Two, "Adult Meditations," includes three meditations for parents and teachers. I adapted these meditations from ones I learned while in Nepal and Tibet. These meditations allow adults to become familiar with the practice of meditation and gives them the confidence and grounding to become better teachers to children by giving adults an opportunity to focus on themselves, others, and the world around them. Part Three, "Children's Meditations," has ten meditations for children organized from simplest to most complex, with each meditation building on the one before.

These meditations teach children that love is always with them. No matter what happens in their lives, once the seed has been planted, the children will have a tool that will always be with them. The "Sunshine Meditation," the "Cleansing Breath Meditation," and the "Catching Blessings Meditation" were created during the tragic events occurring in schools across our country. I wondered how a child could get to such a painful place to commit acts of violence at such a young age. How could I help children not to get to that place? The "Sunshine Meditation" builds self-esteem. It teaches how to breathe in, enlarge and brighten the sunshine ball of love within, and fill the whole self with love. The "OM Meditation" teaches children that love is always within them. The "Cleansing Breath Meditation" teaches children that they can let go of thoughts and feelings that make them feel sad, mad, or bad and that they can instead choose to bring in love, joy, and peace. The "Catching Blessings Meditation" teaches children that love is all around them. It teaches children to look around, prepare, and take hold of and bring within them the love that surrounds them.

The "Inviting the Bell Meditation" teaches the concept of sending and receiving love. I say, "When I strike this bell, the sound it makes will be the sound of my love—how much I love you and how happy I am to be with you." I strike the bell, and we all listen silently until the sound ends.

My home is on an old farm on a lake and we spend many days outside. The "Walking Meditation" started when I was teaching children the importance of being respectful to the trees, plants, insects, and animals and the concept of walking together as a group. Over the years, the children have named different trees and areas on the farm, which we use in this meditation. I blow my Tibetan horn three times and call to the birds, frogs, insects, and rabbits to "get ready; here come the children." We walk together and chant, "Let love guide us," all the way to "Bird Tree" and say, "Thank you, Bird Tree, for taking such great care of the birds." We then walk to "Cattail Bridge" and say, "Thank you, cattails, for keeping us safe and telling us not to come too close because there is water where you are." Next we walk to "Money Tree": "Thank you, Money Tree, for all the gifts of nature." Then we run around the "Circle of Love" (a mowed circle at the end of our path) and chant, "Love is all around us," and stop at "Cobra Crossing" (a stick that looks like a cobra standing in the ground) and say, "Thank you, cobra, for keeping our beach safe." Finally we go to the beach and throw rocks in the water and say a prayer of gratitude for all of nature's gifts.

The "Gratitude Meditation" was created after the birthday party of one of the children. One of the classmates was unhappy that she did not receive gifts or get to blow out the candles, so I wanted to teach the children the importance of being happy for others. We sent gratitude for all the gifts and kind-

■

ness our friend had received on his birthday and we expressed gratitude that he was born. "We are so grateful that our friend Jack was born." I do this meditation on each child's birthday. I feel children learn the joy of being happy for one another and that they learn the joy of knowing how it feels when their friends are happy for them.

The "Singing Bowl Meditation" teaches children about the connection between vibration and sound—the sound and vibration of the bowl and the sound and vibration of the self. A singing bowl placed on the palm of a hand and made to "sing" by circling the rim of the bowl with a wooden striker creates a beautiful sound and tickles the palm. I say, "That is what your love vibration feels and sounds like."

The "Crystal Meditation" teaches positive empowerment. I created this meditation to help children speak in a loving way, touch in a loving way, and think in a loving way. The idea is that we all have love within us and sometimes it gets "stuck" so the crystal helps to get it "unstuck." We do this meditation so that the children will be reminded of speaking, touching, and thinking with love. I hand them the crystal during the day and let them hold it if they did something unkind with their hands. I say, "Hold the crystal until your love is unstuck; you will know when that is because your hands will want to touch in a loving way." They tend to hold the crystal for a minute, concentrating, and then give it back, proclaiming, "My hands are full of love now. I'm ready to touch in a kind and loving way."

The "Rainbow Meditation" was developed after the death of a child's grandparent. Not only did I want to comfort this little boy and the other children, but I wanted to teach them that they could send and receive love to and from anyone, even if someone had died. We created a healing rainbow by starting at the base of our spines and following the ancient seven chakra energy system and its corresponding colors, which runs along the main energy channel parallel to our spines, up to the crowns of our heads. During this meditation, I said, "We are creating our healing rainbow of love—red . . . orange . . . yellow . . . green . . . blue . . . indigo . . . violet—and send it out the tops of our heads. We are sending this rainbow of love to our friend's grandpa who died. Our friend misses his grandpa and his grandpa misses him, too, so let's send the healing rainbow all the way up to heaven to our friend's grandpa." This was a powerful meditation that comforted this child and his friends during this time of grief.

I believe we are all born with everything we need for the life we are living. I believe this book will help children find that place of knowingness and love within themselves. A place that will always be there for them no matter what happens in their lives. A place to calm their fears, build their self-esteem, and find comfort when grieving and in pain. Children will learn to honor and awaken their own spirit within, as well as learn to honor and respect the spirit in others and in the world around them. May the meditations in this book help plant the seed of love and kindness and may they give our precious children a tool that will help this seed grow.

—*Lisa*

PART ONE

Creating Your Space

The ancient traditions of meditation have been around for over 2,500 years. They are carefully respected and honored within this book because they work and are a proven foundation on which to build a meditation practice.

When sitting for meditation for yourself or as a teacher, you need to know your intent. Why are you meditating? What are you teaching? What are you open to learn? Before I meditate I take time to focus on and state my intent—it may be to calm myself, to relax, to focus on a challenge or a project, to acknowledge and clear unwanted thoughts and feelings, to build my confidence, to be more open, to awaken my love within, to fill myself with love, to listen to or to commune with the divine.

Meditation involves the whole child, all of his or her senses and each unique energy and learning style. I have found meditation to fit each learning style: The sounds of the healing music, the bells, the singing bowls, the energy chimes, the Indian rattles, the chants and the mantras, all teach us auditorily. The large bowl placed in the center of the circle, the interesting patterns on the pillows, the sacred items and pictures we use, all teach us visually. The posture we sit in teaches and embraces us kinesthetically, while holding the crystal or feeling the singing bowl vibrating our hand teaches us tactilely. We all have learning styles; one may be more prominent than the other, but we learn through each one. Not only will children learn meditation with their more prominent learning styles, but they will also be given the opportunity to awaken and use their other learning styles.

With the ancient traditional base and the fluidness of meditation, children are encouraged to find that place of love within themselves; this is an opportunity for true empowerment and unlimited inner growth. Children will learn the power of sitting, focusing, and getting in touch with and honoring their inner selves.

Before I teach children meditation, I close my eyes and take three cleansing breaths to clear my mind and let go of my "stuff" so that I can be clean, clear, and "in the moment" to teach. I then state my intent, which may be to awaken the children to the love within and around them, to remind the children to speak, touch, and think with love, to calm the children, to focus the scattered energy of the children, to release a painful, frightening, or confusing thought or feeling, to acknowledge or honor a loss or an unhappy event, to feel joy, or to feel gratitude. I state my intentions aloud.

Setup for group meditation

Tips for a
Successful Meditation

- Speak in a soft, kind, loving voice.
- Smile.
- Be joyful yet serious.
- Store your sacred items on your altar and let the children know that they may not play with them—these objects are not toys.
- Practice the meditations on your own, so you are comfortable.
- At night, use soft lighting.
- Make eye contact when appropriate.
- Do not comment on the way the children breathe.
- Do not comment on whether or not their eyes are open or closed.
- The children will mimic you—the way you speak, how you breathe, how you sit and hold your head, how you hold your hands—so be a good model.
- Place a singing bowl, crystal, picture, or statue in the center of the circle so the children have something to focus on.
- Start with the shorter meditations and progress to the longer meditations.
- Know your intent: What do you want to teach with the meditation and why?

- Gently end a meditation if you feel it is warranted.
- Trust your intuition.
- Be patient; you and the children will look forward to these meditations.

Setting Up Your Space

The Space

Look around your home for a spot that feels quiet, calm, and relaxing. The space should be a reflection and manifestation of your true inner self—calm, uncluttered, clean, orderly, and organized. The space needs to feel peaceful; your eyes, ears, and body need to feel calm and restful. This helps to prepare you for a successful meditation.

The space I use for meditation is in the back of the house. It is a room that is clean and uncluttered, organized for meditation by having meditation pillows and other materials readily available. This is a space where we can hear the music and it is away from the noise of the phone and doorbell.

Choose a spot that the children will feel comfortable in and make sure that the sacred items you use for meditation are kept where the children know not to play with them; they are not to be used as toys. I place my sacred items on a shelf that I call my altar. Make sure you either take the phone off the hook or let the children know that you will not be answering the phone during meditation. Place a note on your door and let the children know that you will not be answering the door during meditation.

Pillows

I place the firm square pillows for the children in a circle along with the larger "teaching pillow" that I sit on. The circle creates a feeling and space of oneness and allows us to have eye contact if needed for instruction.

Children need their own special pillows that they use only for meditation; a firm square pillow gives each child a successful, sure, and comfortable place to sit. There should be enough space between each child so that when the children are in their meditation positions, they do not disturb one another.

Singing Bowl

I place the singing bowl in the center of the circle with a cloth-covered striker. I love the sound of this bowl when it is struck and so do the children. It also gives the children something to focus their eyes on.

When I first meditate with children, especially my eighteen-month to two-year-olds, I find that I strike the bowl more often. This tends to keep their attention focused and they automatically look to the bowl.

Crystal

I place the items I will be using in meditation either in the center of the circle or beside my pillow. I always role-model with the crystal first and pass it in an open palm and offer it to the child on my right.

■

One of the ways a child learns is by touching. Holding a crystal is interesting and different for a child and creates an opportunity for the child to participate in the meditation. The children mimic what I do during the meditation, and when they are finished with the crystal, they offer the child on their right the crystal as I strike the bowl and name the child who is next.

Time

Choose a time of day that works for you and the children. You will need between five and fifteen minutes, depending on the meditation you choose and the number of children. Meditate each day.

Make sure the children are not hungry, thirsty, sick, or too tired. Have them go to the bathroom, or change their diapers before meditation.

Choosing a Meditation

Part Three of this book has ten children's meditations. The easier, shorter meditations are first; they then build on one another and become longer and more complex.

I recommend getting comfortable with meditating yourself first with the adult meditations in Part Two. Read through Part Three, "Children's Meditations." Set up and try out the first meditation without the children;

when you are comfortable and feel ready, teach the first meditation to the children. Then when you are ready, go on to the second meditation. You want to feel familiar and comfortable with each meditation before you teach it to children. Trust your intuition; if you see a meditation that you feel will help a child, learn it, then teach it.

$\mathcal{S}ound$

Sound is vibration and vibration is everywhere, in everything. Vibration has been recognized as a powerful creator and healer since the beginning of time.

Ancient cultures understood the power of vibration and its effects on the human body. Science is now validating these ancient beliefs. Sound has the power to calm and heal the body.

There have been numerous studies on the power of vibration. Studies have shown that calm, soothing music and gentle, loving voices make a positive difference in the health of people, plants, and animals. Studies have also shown that noise pollution creates mental and physical stress, interfering with our ability to sleep well, work productively, and learn effectively.

Many musicians, researchers, and scientists around the world have studied the power of music to calm and heal. Some of the music I play for meditation is the music of Robert Gass and Jonathan Goldman. I believe they understand and use these positive healing vibrational sounds. When choosing music for meditation, ask yourself if the sounds are calming and soothing; do they bring you peace?

I have experienced a difference in my home when I play healing music.

The calm, welcoming, peaceful vibration creates an environment conducive to meditation.

Your voice is vibration. The words you choose and the tone and volume you choose to speak your words in affect your child's energy. A calm, kind, loving voice will attach its energies to the calm, kind, loving energy within a child. Choose the words, the tone, and the volume that create a loving environment for meditation.

I speak in a calm, kind, and loving voice. I play healing music. I use the Indian rattle, the energy chime, bells, and singing bowls with the children. I believe they are healing for the children and make the meditations interesting.

Posture

For over 2,500 years, meditators have used the following posture position. The energies of the body and mind work together. The following position opens the energy channels within the body and allows energy to flow freely throughout the body, helping to free blocked energy. When our channels are open and our energy is allowed to flow freely, we are more able to obtain a clear, open state of mind that will help center us for meditation. I believe this posture position is a powerful tool to have.

The following posture position is described for adults to use during the "Adult Morning Meditation," the "Adult Meditation for World Peace," and the "Adult Meditation for Sending Love to a Child." The modified versions of the posture position for a child are italicized underneath.

Legs and Back

There are three main energy channels running up and down your spine—one on each side of your spine, and one central channel paralleling your spine. When these main channels are open and clear, you are ready for deep contemplation: meditation. Placing a firm pillow underneath your buttocks when crossing your legs will help keep your spine straight so that these main channels will open. In crossing your legs, you are bringing the energy in and guiding it to your main energy channels.

I have the children sit on firm 12 x 12 x 3-inch pillows, with their legs crossed in front of them. I place the pillows in a circle, and as each child sits, I cross the child's legs and I run my hand up and down his or her spine and say, "This is your spine; this is where your energy runs up and down. You need to sit up straight so that your energy can flow up and down easily." As I place my hands on the child's crossed legs, I say, "Your legs need to be crossed so that your spine stays straight so your energy can go up and down." I repeat phrases over and over. I never assume children know or remember from previous meditations. I never want the children to feel as though they do not know what to do or why they are doing it. If I notice a child who is already sitting correctly, I will use this as an opportunity for positive reinforcement. "George, it looks like you are all ready for meditation." As I run my hand up and down his spine, I say, "Your back is nice and straight; now your energy can run up and down easily." As I place my hands on his crossed legs, I say, "Your legs are crossed just right. Now your back can stay straight and your energy can go up and down."

Hands and Arms

You will be creating a circle with your hands and arms. This circle calms and harnesses the energy of your hands and arms. It guides your energy to the main channels, which open you up to a place of calm, clear centeredness. Place your hands, one on top of the other, cupped in your lap. Your right hand, the releasing hand, should be on top of your left hand, the receiving hand, with the tips of your thumbs touching. Bring your elbows slightly out and away from your body, creating a circle.

After I have placed a child's legs and back in the correct position, I place the child's cupped hands, right hand on top of left hand, on his or her lap. This is called the begging bowl position. As I place the child's hands, I say, "I am placing your hands in the begging bowl position, right hand on top of left. Now you can let go of anything sad, mad, or bad you need to let go of and receive your blessings. They will drop right into your begging bowl." As I gently move the child's elbows out, I trace the circle, starting at the begging bowl, with my finger, and then I place my palm on the child's heart and say, "Now all the blessings go right to your heart."

Head and Eyes

Your head needs to bend slightly forward, to allow the three main energy channels to be opened and not blocked. Picture a string being pulled straight up from the top of your spine; you will notice as it is pulled taunt, it straightens your spine and neck, and your head naturally tilts forward. Your eyes may be slightly open, gazing down past the tip of your nose, about twelve to eighteen inches in front of you, or closed.

After setting up the meditation pillows in a circle, I place my singing bowl or sometimes the Buddha statue in the center of the circle. After we are all sitting in position, I say, "Everyone's eyes need to be looking at the singing bowl." This not only gives the children something to do with their eyes, but it also gives them something to concentrate on. Being in a circle equidistant from the bowl, the children naturally tilt their heads forward, allowing their three main channels to open so their energy can flow freely. When I use the Buddha statue, I gesture to each part of the statue as I say, "This is the Buddha; he really knows how to sit. See how straight his back is. See how his legs are crossed. His arms are out and his hands are in the begging bowl position. Look at his eyes; see how he is looking down in front of him, with his head held high. He really knows how to sit. If you forget how to sit, just look at the Buddha and he will remind you what to do." If I notice

■

during meditation a child that needs reminding on how to sit, I gesture with an open hand to the Buddha statue. This helps children to correct themselves, to be successful on their own without feeling criticized. This is very empowering for them.

Jaw and Tongue

Your mouth and jaw should be relaxed, with your teeth slightly apart. Your lips should be gently touching each other. The tip of your tongue should touch the roof of your mouth right behind your front teeth; this completes the connection of the energy flow throughout your body.

I do not comment on jaw and tongue position with preschool children.

Rocking

While observing the Tibetan monks and nuns in Nepal and Tibet, I noticed that while they where chanting, they rocked back and forth, all to their own rhythm and pace. It helps to move and unblock energy.

Before I went to Asia, I had the children rock back and forth. My idea at the time was to mimic the movement of a rocking chair or a mother's rocking, as I believed it brought comfort. The children and I still rock back and forth while we chant, but I know now that it helps move and unblock our energy.

Breath

Breath moves energy. When you are in position and ready to meditate, you need to take three deep cleansing breaths. These cleansing breaths expel your negative energy and bring in good new energy. You will be breathing in and out through your nose. Breathe in through your nose, breathing all the way down to your lower abdomen, relaxing your abdomen, and filling it up like a balloon; then breathe out through your nose, pulling your lower abdomen in and deflating the balloon. Repeat this cleansing breath at least three times. If your mind wanders, gently bring your focus back to your breath. During meditation, slowly breathe gently in and out of your nose all the way down to your lower abdomen.

The children mimic what I do. I model and teach during our cleansing breath to breathe in through the nose and out through the mouth. I do not comment on how a child is breathing, as most preschoolers tend to breathe in and out of their mouths, especially when they have a stuffy nose.

Tips for Setting Up Your Space— Checklist

- Take your phone off the hook.
- If needed, put a "please do not disturb" note on your door.
- Choose where you will meditate; pick a spot where you will have the least distractions.
- Know your intent—what you want to teach and why.
- Decide which meditation you want to do and look it over.
- Put on your meditation music.
- Place your meditation pillows on the floor, across from each other or in a circle if there are more than two of you.
- Place your singing bowl, energy chime, Indian rattle, crystal, or whatever tool(s) you need for your meditation of choice and place it in between the two pillows, beside your pillow, or in the center of the circle.
- As you strike your bowl or chime, let the children know "it's meditation time."
- Sit cross-legged on your meditation pillows, and begin.

Terms, Materials, and Illustrations

Walker in begging bowl position—three years old

Terms, Materials, and Illustrations

$\mathcal{T}$he following terms, materials, and illustrations are what I use when meditating with children. They are reflective of my interest in the Tibetan Buddhist, Hindu, and Native American meditations and cultures. These ancient cultures understand energy—the energy of our earth, our bodies, and our minds. They understand the power in sacred sounds and they bless and empower their sacred items to enhance their meditations, ceremonies, and lives. They honor and allow the sacred into their lives every day.

I consider the items I use with the children blessed and sacred; they are placed on a shelf, my altar, in the room we meditate in. We have empowerment ceremonies when the children make their own sacred items. As with the power stick (see page 34), we empower these items to bring the children what they need in a kind and loving way: "May this power stick bring Greer all she needs in a kind and loving way."

The sacred sound of "OM" is considered by many to be the mantra of creation. In the Tibetan Buddhist tradition, the sanskrit word "OM" written "AUM" represents and vibrates to the body, speech, and mind. It is used in many Tibetan chants and mantras, the most popular in Tibet being "*Aum Mani Padmae Hum*," a chant for world peace. The "OM" Meditation in Part

Three has a chant the children and I sing every day: "Ommm, I love my home, I love my mom, I love my dad. Ommm, I love my home, I love my mom, I love my dad. Ommm, I love my home, I love my mom, I love my dad, Ommm, Ommm, Ommm." It is a powerful chant and mantra for children. I happen to feel it is a powerful chant and mantra for adults, too. Try it!

While I traveled in Nepal and Tibet, I came to love the greeting *"Namaste."* Both of your hands are placed together with the thumbs tucked in and placed over your heart chakra, and with a slight gentle bow of your head and upper body, you say, *"Namaste,"* while making eye contact. This greeting means "From my jewel within me, my place of love, to your jewel within you, your place of love." I begin and end my meditations with this greeting, saying, *"Namaste,"* to each child. You may choose to include this in your meditations. When we are done with our meditations, I place my hand on each child's heart and say, "We all have a jewel within us that shines with love and it is right here!"

Terms Used in This Book

Begging bowl position—Place your hands cupped on your lap, right hand placed on top of the left hand, with tips of thumbs touching, creating a bowl. Bring your elbows slightly out and away from your body creating a circle. Right hand is releasing hand; left hand is receiving hand.

Being in the moment—Putting all other thoughts and activities aside and being present with the person or activity you are with at that moment.

Chakra—An energy center in the body.

The Seven Chakra Centers

- Violet—7th Chakra—connection with the divine—top of head—Crown Chakra
- Indigo—6th Chakra—intuition—third eye/forehead—Brow Chakra
- Blue—5th Chakra—communication—Throat Chakra
- Green—4th Chakra—love—Heart Chakra
- Yellow—3rd Chakra—individuality—Solar Plexus Chakra
- Orange—2nd Chakra—creativity—below belly button—Sacral Chakra
- Red—1st Chakra—your roots—base of spine—Base Chakra

Chant—A repetition of sacred words and sounds that vibrates within and around the energy centers.

Circle of light—All things become love when surrounded in a circle of light.

Gratitude—Thankful appreciation.

Intent—The goal upon which your mind is fixed.

Mantra—Sacred words of great power and blessings.

Mudra—Symbolic hand gestures used in Hindu and Tibetan Buddhist ceremony and prayer.

"Namaste"—A sacred greeting honoring the spirit within, meaning "From my jewel within me, my place of love, to your jewel within you, your place of love."

"OM"—The mantra of creation (spelled AUM in Tibetan); "OM" awakens and connects us to love.

Prayer—Spiritual communication.

Sacred space—Everywhere is sacred; it is anywhere you feel at peace.

Spiritual—Of the spirit or the soul; the intellect.

Vibration—Everything and everyone has a vibration; feelings, thoughts, words, music, trees, all of nature—everything.

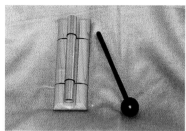

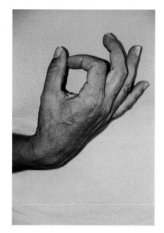

Starting at the top, left to right:

Rose quartz crystals, Singing bowl, Incense and sage,
Energy chime, Meditation pillow, Power stick,
Prayer wheel, Mudra for teaching, Indian rattle,
Thongka, Altar, Prayer flags

Starting at the top, left to right:
Three begging bowl positions
Saige opening her heart, throat, and mind for love
Mom and child using energy chime, Indian rattle, and singing bowl
Mom and child meditating, Group setup, Mom and child sending love

Materials Used in This Book

Meditation pillows—12 x 12 x 3-inch pillows

Indian rattle—12-inch stick covered in leather, beads, and feathers, with a hard leather ball at the end filled with dried corn kernels.

Rose quartz crystal—3 x 4-inch crystal, smoothed.

Singing bowl—Mine is a 5 x 1-inch metal bowl with a 7-inch wooden striker covered in leather, sitting on a 6 x 3-inch round cushion.

Single-tone bell—My energy chime is a 5-inch tube with a 6-inch wooden striker.

Background Music—All *On Wings of Song* CDs by Robert Gass; *Om Sanctuary* from JDM Music; Tibetan incantations and Tibetan Buddhist chants; CDs by Jonathan Goldman.

Parenting and Teaching to a Child's Spirit

Walker, three years old, and his mom, Cheryl, making a power stick

$\mathcal{T}$he following creative ideas and crafts are ones that I use with children. These were chosen because of my interest in Tibetan Buddhist, Hindu, and Native American meditations and cultures. The children enjoy making these crafts and continue to use them for years after they are made. I believe items made by children are empowered with love.

Each meditation within this book has a "Creative Ideas" page. Those "Creative Ideas" pages and the following "Creative Ideas and Crafts" section are for after you have taken the time to learn and practice the traditions of meditation that are known to work. Set a foundation in the traditions of meditation, with posture and breathing; create a clean, calm space, organized with healing music and sacred items; create an altar on which to place your sacred items; and become familiar and comfortable with the words and terms. In time, you will be ready to introduce your own ideas and crafts!

Creative Ideas and Crafts

Altar

A place created for keeping your "sacred" items.

Use a table, shelf, or top of a bureau near your child's bed. Choose a spot that your child can see as he or she falls asleep. Then together place on it the treasures you and your child have collected: stones, pinecones, pictures of loved ones, anything important to your child. You can make your own altar from a box or crate, and paint and decorate it with loving thoughts, pictures, and trinkets. You can decorate a piece of cloth to place on top. This altar will bring your child comfort while falling asleep or if he or she awakens in the night. It will start and end your child's days with loving comfort.

Being in the Moment

Putting all other thoughts and activities aside and really being with the person or activity you are with at that moment.

Have a bell in your home and teach your family that when they hear the sound of the bell, you are stopping and thinking of them and how much you love them and how happy you are to be with them. Create a special time of day that becomes the quiet, meditative time for you and your family.

Circle of Light

A circle of light is created in your mind's eye during meditation. Only love is allowed in the circle of light; everything in the circle of light changes to love.

Take a moment to close your eyes and picture your child circled in light when he or she goes to sleep at night or goes off to school. Circle your child's school in light, circle your home, yourself; anyone and anything can be circled in this loving light.

Crystals

Crystals have vibration, energy. I use the rose quartz crystal with the children, as it is full of love energy.

Take your child to a shop to choose his or her own crystal. Give children crystals as gifts with cards telling what the crystal means.

Place your crystal(s) on your altar and use it with meditations. If your child is having a difficult time expressing him- or herself, ask your child to hold the crystal up to his or her throat for a few moments to help "open the throat up for loving words."

Give a crystal, such as a rose quartz crystal, to your child to take with him or her on a new adventure like starting school. You can "fill the crystal with love" and send it with your child. Remember: Small crystals are a choking hazard. Choose large ones.

Gratitude

Statements of gratitude can be said throughout the day.

Start your day with a statement of gratitude.

Let your child know you are grateful that he or she was born and is a part of your life.

Have your child make a picture book of what he or she is grateful for. Make a book of gratitude of what you are grateful for.

Incense

Incense clears the space you are in and sends love out into the world.

I burn my incense during my own meditation, before the children arrive; I do not burn incense during meditation with young children.

I do home blessings with children in which we walk around the house, inside and out, as I carry a stick of smoking sage, clearing the way for love to come in.

Indian Rattle

Used by Native Americans. Use this to give and receive blessings for yourself, others, your home—anyone and anything that wants or needs a blessing.

Create an Indian rattle out of a stick or wooden dowel. Decorate the stick with paint, feathers, beads (age appropriate), and ribbons. Paint and decorate a baby rattle and attach it to the end of your stick. Have a ceremony to bless the Indian rattle to bring only love.

Mantra

Sacred words of great power and blessings. Saying a mantra over and over throughout your day brings positive energy and change.

Choose a positive statement or goal for each day, week, and/or year. Write each mantra on a card, decorate the card, and hang the card on your mirror, refrigerator, car visor, door, or altar to help remind you and keep you focused on loving thoughts and deeds. Say these mantras first thing in the morning and throughout your day.

Meditation Pillow

A pillow used to sit on during meditation.

Create your own meditation pillow. Cover a pillow in muslin, use fabric pens or paint, then sew or glue on trinkets and treasures to personalize your pillow.

Use any pillow, folded blanket, rug, or chair. I use firm 12 x 12 x 3-inch pillows for the children.

Mudra

Much like sign language, these sacred hand gestures are used in Tibetan Buddhist and Hindu ceremonies and prayers. I use Tibetan Buddhist mudras for signaling patience and signaling a new teaching. Children enjoy these signals and it is a silent way to give direction.

Make up your own family hand signals for "I love you," "Think 'kindness,'" "Have a great day," "Quiet, please," "Patience," "Time to go." These are great to use at church and restaurants and when visiting relatives and friends.

Power Stick

This stick brings powerful, positive energy while held in your hand as you speak your mantra or your positive affirmation.

Pick a stick that feels good in your hand as you stretch your arm out straight. Decorate this stick with crystals, feathers, beads (age appropriate), and colored yarns. Wrap the "handle" of your stick with yarn or rawhide strips. Have a ceremony saying, "May this power stick bring only love." I use the power stick with children when powerful love is needed.

Prayer

Before lunch, we say a prayer of gratitude for our food, our families, each child, and our day.

Let children create their own prayers. Use this time to thank a child for a loving act or to encourage loving acts, to remember what you and they are grateful for, and to send healing love to friends, family, and the world.

Prayer Flags

Prayers for world peace are written on red, blue, green, yellow, and white square pieces of cloth, strung on long strings, and hung all over Tibetan communities. The energy of the prayer goes out into the world as the wind blows.

You can buy these or make your own. Cut out squares of colored cloth and write your own loving prayers for yourself, others, and the world around you. Hang these prayer flags in your child's room, outside his or her window, in your yard, or by your child's outdoor play area. They make great gifts.

Prayer Wheels

The mantra Aum Mani Padmae Hum, a Tibetan prayer for world peace, is written thousands of times and placed within a cylinder on a stick. Each time this cylinder turns, these prayers for world peace go out into the world.

Create a prayer wheel by placing your prayers for world peace in a decorated bowl or jar that you can spin or roll, so your prayers for world peace will go out into the world. Decorate a wind chime with prayers for world peace. Hang it where you can see and hear it.

Sacred Space

A place inside or out that makes you feel at peace—everywhere is sacred.

Find a spot in or around your home—your bedroom, your child's room, your living room, garden, or porch—and create your own sacred space for meditating, quiet time, family talks.

Singing Bowl

A metal bowl with a wooden striker covered in leather. When the bowl's rim is circled with the striker, the bowl vibrates, or "sings."

Test the metal bowls in your home with a wooden dowel to see if they sing, or you can buy a singing bowl and striker at a local Asian or spiritual shop.

Single-Tone Bell

A single-tone energy chime mounted on a wooden base rung with a wooden striker. These come in many varieties and sizes. Choose the sound that resonates with you.

Use any bell that sounds pleasing to your ear.

Teach the children in your life to stop and listen to the sound of the bell. Teach them to listen until they can no longer hear the chime. You can use this to change the energy of the moment.

Ring the bell at different times of the day. When the bell rings, teach the children to take this time to appreciate whom they are with and appreciate what they are doing.

Thongkas

These are paintings used in Tibetan meditation. They are sacred pictures and designs painted with crushed gems on yak hide that are lovingly empowered.

Create your own meditation paintings with loving pictures, designs, and colors that resonate with you. You can also create one by cutting out pictures that bring you peace and gluing them on paper to hang in a sacred spot.

Vibration

Everyone and everything has a vibration—feelings, thoughts, words, music, animals, trees, food—all of nature, everything.

Have your child touch the side of a washing machine when it is on the spin cycle so he or she can learn about and feel vibration; put a glass of water on a speaker when music is playing so your child can see vibration; play different styles of music and observe how vibration affects your child.

PART TWO

Adult
Meditations

Adult Morning
Meditation

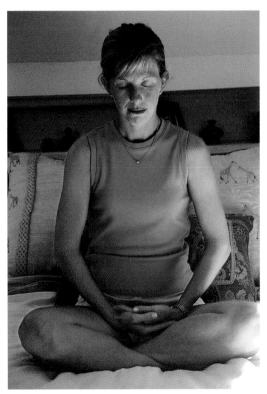

Aimee—mother of two-year-old Avery and one-year-old Nathan

Adult Morning
Meditation

"It's not that what you are saying is new,
it is that you reminded me how important
it is to teach love and kindness to my child;
now I have a tool to help remind me."

—Kathleen, mother of a three-year-old

Introduction

You are the teacher. Children learn from your every word, every touch, every act and deed, each minute of each day. All time is quality time with children. They love you and look to you to teach them. You need to be the best teacher you can be. What do you want to teach them? This is the childhood they will base and build their life on.

When you have young children in your life, the pace is fast, busy, and demanding. As a parent, teacher, grandparent, or health-care provider, you need to take time for yourself—time to be quiet, to breathe slowly, and to go within, staying in touch with and honoring your own spirit. You need to remind yourself to be grateful and to give thanks for your life, the children in your life, your family, and all that you have. This is a gift you can give to yourself each day.

The following meditation will help you take the time to be kind to yourself and to be grateful for the ones that you love and all that you have. It will prepare you to plant the seed of love and kindness within each child in your life.

Creative Ideas

Materials

Meditation pillow—any pillow, folded blanket, rug; any spot you create inside or outside.

Terms

"Breathe in love/joy/peace"—use any positive, loving word.

"Breathe out sadness/anger/badness"—use any negative word.

"Visualize bright white/golden light"—visualize any color light that feels warm and loving to you.

"Visualize in your mind's eye"—use pictures if needed.

Uses

Use this meditation any time of the day—in your home, in your car while you are waiting for your child to get out of school or activities.

Use in doctors' and dentists' waiting rooms.

Use anywhere and anytime you are feeling drained.

■

Your Own Creative Ideas

Adult Morning Meditation

This meditation gives adults an opportunity to honor and acknowledge with gratitude their love for themselves, the children and families in their lives, their homes, and all they have.

Materials
- Meditation pillow

Sit on your meditation pillow or on your bed with your legs crossed, or you may choose to sit on a chair with your feet placed firmly on the floor. Sit with your back straight. Place your hands in the begging bowl position with your eyes open, gazing past the tip of your nose, or with your eyes closed.

■

As you begin, say aloud or to yourself: "I am surrounded in light and love."

State your intent, such as: "To see with love."
(Slowly breathe in and out through your nose until you feel relaxed and ready to begin.)

"Breathe in love."
(Slow, deep breath in)

"Breathe out sadness."
(Slow, deep breath out)

"Breathe in joy."
(Slow, deep breath in)

"Breathe out anger."
(Slow, deep breath out)

"Breathe in peace."
(Slow, deep breath in)

"Breathe out badness."
(Slow, deep breath out)

"All of my sadness, anger, and badness changes to bright white sparkles of love."

■

Be in the moment: Give gratitude for a new day.

Continue taking slow, deep breaths, and when you are ready, continue. . . .

Visualize a bright white light above your head—this is a healing, loving light.

Now, with each breath you take, visualize this flowing light pouring slowly throughout your body—like filling a vessel with syrup from top to bottom. Follow your intuition: If you feel you need more loving light in one area, take as many breaths as you need until you feel ready to continue.

Breathe this healing, loving light in through the top of your head. With each breath, begin to feel this warm, loving light filling your body with love—first behind your eyes . . . now behind your nose . . . behind your ears . . . down through your throat . . . pouring into your heart . . . down your arms . . . into your hands . . . to your fingers . . . now slowly down your spine . . .into your sitting bones . . . down your thighs . . . into your knees . . . down your calves . . . into your ankles . . . into your feet . . . to your toes. . . . Now with each breath, feel this loving light expanding throughout your entire body. You are now filled with healing, loving light.

Be in the moment: Give gratitude for your life.

Now, for a few breaths, breathe this bright white healing, loving, light through the crown of your head into your heart chakra. With each breath in, feel your heart chakra expanding and filling up with love.

■

In your mind's eye, picture the children and family members in your life sitting facing you. . . . Continue to breathe in this bright white loving light. . . . Bring each child and family member forward one at a time. . . . As you breathe out, send this loving light out from your heart chakra to each of the children's and family member's heart chakra, filling each with love.

Spend as much time as you feel you need with each person. Trust your intuition. Repeat this for each person.

Be in the moment: Give gratitude for all the children and family members in your life.

Picture in your mind's eye your home. Continue to breathe in the bright white loving light through the crown of your head. . . . As you breathe out, send a ribbon of this light from your heart chakra throughout and around your home, filling your home with love.

Be in the moment: Give gratitude for your home.

When you are ready, continue. . . .

"Breathe in love."
(Slow, deep breath in)

"Breathe out sadness."
(Slow, deep breath out)

■

"Breathe in joy."
(Slow, deep breath in)

"Breathe out anger."
(Slow, deep breath out)

"Breathe in peace."
(Slow, deep breath in)

"Breathe out badness."
(Slow, deep breath out)

"All of my sadness, anger, and badness changes to bright white sparkles of love."

Be in the moment: Give gratitude for all that you have.

Mantra: "I have everything I need to be loving to my family and the children in my life."

Adult Meditation for World Peace

Nicole—mother of three-year-old Sophia and one-year-old Max

Adult Meditation for World Peace

Introduction

While watching a live broadcast from the Middle East after September 11, 2001, the camera focused in on a group of men. I noticed in the background a father walking his son home from school. Hand in hand they walked, the boy, looking like a second grader, dressed neatly in shorts and a sweater, schoolbag in hand. It could have been any father and son, on their way home from school in any country. All of a sudden, the group of men being filmed began throwing rocks over a fence, their faces full of anger as they yelled and hurled the rocks. Soon the father let go of his son's hand and joined the men hurling rocks, as his young son watched in stillness. The boy then dropped his schoolbag, ran to join his dad, picked up a rock, and started to yell and throw rocks alongside his father.

I watched as the seed of hate and fear was planted in a child that day. Adults plant seeds every day. Are you planting the seed of hate and fear or are you planting the seed of love and kindness?

May the following meditation help you plant the seeds of love, tolerance, and peace within you, the children in your life, your community, your country, and the world.

Creative Ideas

Materials

Meditation pillow—any pillow, folded blanket, rug; any spot you create inside or outside.

Terms

"Breathe in love/joy/peace"—use any positive, loving word.

"Breathe out sadness/anger/badness"—use any negative word.

"Visualize bright white/golden light"—visualize any color light that feels warm and loving to you.

"Visualize in your mind's eye"—use pictures if needed.

Uses

Trust your intuition—send love and light to anyone who is on your mind.

Send love and light to someone who is ill, away from home, or going through a difficult time.

Create a peaceful environment before company arrives.

Send love and light to someone you are having difficulties with.

■

Your Own Creative Ideas

Adult Meditation for World Peace

This meditation was adapted from a meditation I learned at Kopan Monestary in Kathmandu, Nepal. This meditation gives adults an opportunity to acknowledge and honor all adults in the world. To create a peaceful, loving world for our children will take all adults, from all walks of life, from all religious backgrounds. No matter what the color of our skin or what our beliefs, we will all need to raise the children in our lives with love, tolerance, and respect for themselves, others, and the world around them.

Materials
- Meditation pillow

■

Sit on your meditation pillow or on your bed with your legs crossed, or you may choose to sit on a chair with your feet placed firmly on the floor. Sit with your back straight. Place your hands in the begging bowl position with your eyes open, gazing past the tip of your nose, or with your eyes closed.

As you begin, say aloud or to yourself: "I am surrounded in light and love."

State your intent, such as: "I dedicate this meditation to world peace."
(Slowly breathe in and out through your nose until you feel relaxed and ready to begin.)

"Breathe in love."
(Slow, deep breath in)

"Breathe out sadness."
(Slow, deep breath out)

"Breathe in joy."
(Slow, deep breath in)

"Breathe out anger."
(Slow, deep breath out)

"Breathe in peace."
(Slow, deep breath in)

■

"Breathe out badness."
(Slow, deep breath out)

"All of my sadness, anger, and badness changes to bright white sparkles of love."

Be in the moment for a few slow, deep breaths.

Visualize and feel a bright white loving light in your heart chakra.

Now, with each slow, deep breath in, feel this loving light growing. With each breath in, your whole body is filling with this loving light. You are just like the sun—your whole body is radiating this bright white loving light from within, shining out all around you.

Be in the moment for a few slow, deep breaths.

Now, in your mind's eye, gather all the adults in your neighborhood and sit them in front of you. As you breathe in, fill your heart chakra with this loving light. As you breathe out, send this loving light out in shining rays from your heart chakra into all of their heart chakras.

Be in the moment for a few slow, deep breaths, growing this bright white loving light within your heart chakra.

Now, in your mind's eye, gather all the adults in your community and sit them in front of you. As you breathe in, fill your heart chakra with this loving light. As you

■

breathe out, send this loving light out in shining rays from your heart chakra into all of their heart chakras.

Be in the moment for a few slow, deep breaths, growing this bright white loving light within your heart chakra.

Now, in your mind's eye, gather all the adults in your country and sit them in front of you. As you breathe in, fill your heart chakra with this loving light. As you breathe out, send this loving light out in shining rays from your heart chakra into all of their heart chakras.

Be in the moment for a few slow, deep breaths, growing this bright white loving light within your heart chakra.

Now, in your mind's eye, gather all the adults in the world and sit them in front of you. As you breathe in, fill your heart chakra with this loving light. As you breathe out, send this loving light out in shining rays from your heart chakra into all of their heart chakras.

Be in the moment for a few slow, deep breaths, growing this bright white loving light within your heart chakra.

Now, as you breathe in, continue to fill your heart chakra with this loving light. As you breathe out, visualize all the adults dispersing as they become bright white sparkles of loving light.

■

When you are ready, continue. . . .

"Breathe in love."
(*Slow, deep breath in*)

"Breathe out sadness."
(*Slow, deep breath out*)

"Breathe in joy."
(*Slow, deep breath in*)

"Breathe out anger."
(*Slow, deep breath out*)

"Breathe in peace."
(*Slow, deep breath in*)

"Breathe out badness."
(*Slow, deep breath out*)

"All of my sadness, anger, and badness changes to bright white sparkles of love."

Be in the moment for a few slow, deep breaths.

Mantra: "May *all* adults of the world be happy."

Adult Meditation
for Sending Love
to a Child

Dan and five-day-old daughter, Lucie

Adult Meditation
for Sending Love
to a Child

"I was unable to totally bond with my child;
I had a fear I was going to lose him."

— *Nicole, mother of a premature baby*

Introduction

*H*aving an ill child in your life is stressful, difficult, and heart wrenching. The inability to fix what is wrong can make you feel useless, helpless, and hopeless. The fear of losing your child can cloud the bond of love that you and he or she needs. Bonding is what makes us compassionate, loving human beings. What do we do when we feel unable to connect because of fear and the inability to "fix" a child or the inability to physically hold him or her because of distance or hospital apparatus?

■

The following meditation was developed after I had met with a pediatric intensive care unit doctor and nurse and the mother of a very ill child. They all spoke of the challenge to create and keep a bond with a critically ill newborn and the painful disconnection that can happen when a child is diagnosed with a chronic illness or when a child is in a life-threatening situation. The inability to touch and hold the child along with the fear of losing him or her can create a detachment.

May the following meditation help acknowledge and strengthen the bond of love for those in need.

Creative Ideas

Materials

Chair or bed—any spot you can sit comfortably.

Terms

"Breathe in love/peace"—use any positive, loving word.

"Breathe out fear/sadness/anger/pain"—use any negative word that resonates with your situation.

"Visualize in your mind's eye"—use pictures if needed.

"Mommy/Daddy loves you"—use siblings, family members, any positive statement.

■

Uses

Use this meditation when your child is away from you or when you are having difficulties with your child.

Use with adults who are ill.

Use when you are pregnant or with your newborn.

Your Own Creative Ideas

Adult Meditation for Sending Love to a Child

This meditation gives adults who have a chronically ill child, a child in a life-threatening situation, or a critically ill newborn a tool to help acknowledge and empower the bond of love.

■

Sit comfortably on a chair or bed with your back straight. Place your hands in the begging bowl position or rest them gently on your lap, with your eyes open or closed.

As you begin, say aloud or to yourself: "I am surrounded in light and love."

State your intent, such as: "I dedicate this meditation to the love within all of us." (*Slowly breathe in and out through your nose until you feel relaxed and ready to begin.*)

"Breathe in love."
(*Slow, deep breath in*)

"Breathe out fear."
(*Slow, deep breath out*)

"Breathe in love."
(*Slow, deep breath in*)

"Breathe out sadness."
(*Slow, deep breath out*)

"Breathe in love."
(*Slow, deep breath in*)

"Breathe out pain."
(*Slow, deep breath out*)

■

"All of my fear, sadness, and pain changes to bright white healing, loving light."

Be in the moment for a few slow, deep breaths.

Visualize and feel a bright white healing, loving light surrounding you.

Visualize your child surrounded in this bright white healing, loving light.

Now, as you continue breathing, picture in your mind's eye this bright white healing, loving light above your head. Open the crown chakra at the top of your head and as you breathe in, this loving light travels with each breath—behind your eyes, behind your nose, down your throat, and into your heart chakra—traveling into your heart chakra until it is full of this loving light from above.

Be in the moment for a few slow, deep breaths.

In your mind's eye, visualize this bright white healing, loving light in your child's heart chakra.

Be in the moment for a few slow, deep breaths.

Opening your heart chakra, send this bright white healing, loving light from your heart chakra to your child's heart chakra, filling your child with this loving light.

Be in the moment for a few slow, deep breaths.

As you continue breathing, feel the loving light of the child's heart chakra joining the loving light of your heart chakra.

Be in the moment for a few slow, deep breaths.

As you breathe, feel the power of love as it bonds and heals both you and your child.

Be in the moment for a few slow, deep breaths.

When you are ready, send positive words of healing and love—"I love you," "Mommy loves you," "Daddy loves you," "Grandma and Grandpa love you," "So many people love you."...

Be in the moment for a few slow, deep breaths.

Breathe in and allow the love of your child to speak to you.

Be in the moment for a few slow, deep breaths.

Picture in your mind's eye holding, caressing, and loving your child, surrounded in this bright white healing, loving light.

Be in the moment and when you are ready, continue....

"Breathe in love."
(Slow, deep breath in)

"Breathe out fear."
(Slow, deep breath out)

"Breathe in love."
(Slow, deep breath in)

"Breathe out sadness."
(Slow, deep breath out)

"Breathe in peace."
(Slow, deep breath in)

"Breathe out anger."
(Slow, deep breath out)

"All of my fear, sadness, and anger changes to a flowing ribbon of bright white healing, loving light."

Be in the moment for a few slow, deep breaths.

Mantra: "We are all surrounded in bright white healing, loving light."

PART THREE

Children's Meditations

Sunshine
Meditation

Weller—two years old

Sunshine Meditation

Introduction

*H*opefully, you have all had those moments of feeling like a puffed-up peacock, strutting along, feeling just a little taller, a little lighter, a little happier, and everything seems to be right in your world.

When children are feeling this way, they look and feel just like a piece of sunshine. You want to be around them and bask in their joy and inhale the love they emit.

This meditation teaches children how to get in touch with their place of love within themselves and how to grow that love whenever they need it.

Creative Ideas

Materials

Meditation pillow—any pillow, folded blanket, rug; any spot you create inside or outside.

Terms

"Ball of sunshine light/ball of love/energy ball of love."

■

Uses

Use this meditation when a child needs to feel comfortable in a new or uncomfortable situation.

Use right before family or friends come to visit, or in the car on the way to visit family or friends.

Use in the morning before school.

Use this meditation yourself. It takes only a minute and has great rewards for both you and the children in your life. It can easily be done on the go— anywhere, anytime.

Your Own Creative Ideas

Sunshine Meditation

This meditation teaches children how to create and build their own self-esteem and how to fill themselves up with love from within.

Materials

- Meditation pillows

Arrange the meditation pillows in a circle.

"We are going to sit with our legs crossed, our backs straight, and our heads held high. Our hands are placed crossed over our heart chakras."

"May this circle be surrounded in light and love."

State your intent, such as: "To fill yourself with love from within."

"Beneath your crossed hands is a ball of sunshine light, which is full of love. Every time you breathe in, your ball of sunshine light gets bigger and bigger and bigger. Now we are going to fill ourselves up with this bright ball of sunshine light, which is full of love."

"Now we are going to breathe in and make our ball of sunshine light grow bigger."
(Long exaggerated breath in, long exaggerated breath out)

"And bigger."
(Long exaggerated breath in, long exaggerated breath out)

"And bigger."
(Long exaggerated breath in, long exaggerated breath out)

"Can you feel yourself all filled up with love?"

"Now we are all bright balls of sunshine light."

Mantra: "We *are* sunshine love."

"OM" Meditation

Avery—two years old

"OM" Meditation

"Hannah, you need to go and sleep in your own bed;
Daddy can't fall asleep. 'Daddy, if you can't sleep,
put your hand on your heart and do, "Ommm."'"

—*Father of two-year-old Hannah*

Introduction

When I first introduce this meditation, I sit cross-legged with the child cross-legged in my lap. I place the child's hands with mine over his or her heart chakra. I rock back and forth and, in a singsong voice, chant, "Ommm, Ommm, Ommm." I invite the child to chant with me. As the child begins chanting, I say, "Can you feel that tickling on your hand? That is love's vibration."

The vibration of "OM" is love; it is in everything, in everyone, and everywhere. "OM" is the same sound as the 'om' in *home*. We chant, "Ommm, I love my home, I love my mom, I love my dad, Ommm, Ommm, Ommm."

When a child misses his or her parents, I say, "Put your hand on your heart chakra and chant, "Ommm." Do you feel that love vibration? Even though your mom and dad are not here right now, their love is always with you. Anytime you need to feel your mom and dad's love, it is right there in

■

your heart always. You have so many people who love you, and all that love is right there in your heart." This teaches children that they can tap into that love and comfort themselves whenever they need it.

Creative Ideas

Materials

Meditation pillow—any pillow, folded blanket, rug; any spot you create inside or outside.

Terms

"Heart chakra"—heart.

"Love vibration"—love energy.

"Chant"—sing.

"Mom/Dad"—friends', family members', names.

Uses

Use this meditation anytime a child needs to feel comforted.

Use before meals or at bedtime.

Use to teach children how they can calm themselves when they are afraid or hurt.

Use before doctor, dentist, and hospital visits.

Use in the morning before school.

Use to calm children when they miss a parent or anyone important to them.

Use when a child misses a loved one who has passed on.

Your Own Creative Ideas

"OM" Meditation

This meditation teaches children that love is always inside of them, and that whenever they need it, they can tap into that love.

Materials

* Meditation pillows

Arrange the meditation pillows in a circle.

"We are going to sit with our legs crossed, our backs straight, and our heads held high. Our hands are in the begging bowl position."

∎

"May this circle be surrounded in light and love."

State your intent, such as: "To show that love is always with you."

"'OM' is the sound of love. It is what love sounds like. 'OM' is inside of every-thing and everyone. Love is everywhere. The sound of 'OM' is in the word *home*. Home, Ommm . . . Ommm . . . Ommm . . . home. Can you hear that? Home is a place of love."

"We can wake up our love vibration by chanting, 'Ommm.' We will put our hands on our heart chakras, rock back and forth, and chant, 'Ommm, Ommm, Ommm.'"

"Can you feel your hands getting tickled? That is your love vibration. Everyone and everything has a love vibration. Everyone who loves you—your mom, your dad, your grandma and grandpa—their love is always with you even if they are not. Love is always with you. Anytime you feel sad, mad, or bad and you want to wake up and feel your love vibration, put your hands over your heart chakra and chant, 'Ommm, Ommm, Ommm,' and you will feel your love vibration."

"Now we will rock back and forth and sing the Ommm chant three times."

Chant the following in a singsong voice:

"Ommm, I love my home, I love my mom, I love my dad . . ."

■

"Ommm, I love my home, I love my mom, I love my dad . . ."

"Ommm, I love my home, I love my mom, I love my dad . . ."

"Ommm, Ommm, Ommm."

Mantra: "Love is *always* with us."

Cleansing Breath Meditation

Lisa teaching meditation to two- and three-year-olds

Cleansing Breath Meditation

Introduction

*T*hink of a time when you calmed yourself by taking a few deep breaths or calmed a child by saying, "Slow down and take a few deep breaths." You look in the child's eyes and you breathe together until he or she is calm.

The cleansing breath is similar; it is a long, deep breath in (through the nose, for adults), all the way to the lower abdomen, and a long breath out (through the mouth) until all the air is out. Children mimic what you do. Don't comment. Preschoolers tend to breathe in and out through their mouths. It is about them becoming aware of the power of their own breath.

The children's parents and I use the "Cleansing Breath Meditation" many different ways. We use it when a child needs to be calmed, to rid a child of fearful thoughts and feelings, to help a child face a new situation or to gather his or her thoughts. It has been used in cars, planes, and boats, at doctors', dentists', and hospitals. It can be used anytime and anywhere. I use it at the beginning and end of many of my meditations with the children.

■

Creative Ideas

Materials

Meditation pillow—any pillow, folded blanket, rug; any spot you create inside or outside.

Singing bowl—any metal bowl, bell, or single-tone energy chime.

Striker—wooden spoon or dowel.

Terms

"Breathe in love/joy/peace"—use any positive, loving word.

"Breathe out sadness/madness/badness"—use any negative word.

Uses

Use this meditation to help a child relieve stress.

Use anytime a child needs to be calmed or focused.

Use when a child has awoken from a bad dream.

Use to calm a child in a new or frightening situation.

Use this meditation anytime, anywhere, as a quick, easy, very powerful tool for a young child to learn.

■

Your Own Creative Ideas

Cleansing Breath Meditation

This meditation teaches children that they can release negative feelings and thoughts and replace them with positive feelings and thoughts.

Materials
- Meditation pillows
- Singing bowl
- Striker

Arrange the meditation pillows in a circle with the singing bowl and striker in the center.

■

"We are going to sit with our legs crossed, our backs straight, and our heads held high. Our hands are in the begging bowl position and our eyes are looking at the bowl in the center of the circle."

Strike the bowl.

Listen until the bowl quiets.

"May this circle be surrounded in light and love."

State your intent, such as: "We are letting go of sad, mad, and bad feelings and replacing them with love, joy, and peace."

"I'm going to strike the bowl and we will breathe three times. The first breath we will breathe in will be love."

Strike the bowl.

"Breathe in love."
(Long exaggerated breath in through the nose)

"Breathe out sadness."
(Long exaggerated breath out through the mouth)

Strike the bowl.

∎

"Breathe in joy."
(Long exaggerated breath in through the nose)

"Breathe out madness."
(Long exaggerated breath out through the mouth)

Strike the bowl.

"Breathe in peace."
(Long exaggerated breath in through the nose)

"Breathe out badness."
(Long exaggerated breath out through the mouth)

"All the sadness, madness, and badness changes to bright white sparkles of love."

Mantra: "We are full of love, joy, and peace today."

Catching Blessings Meditation

Avery, two years old, catching blessings from her mom, Aimee

Catching Blessings Meditation

Introduction

$\mathcal{W}$e are all truly blessed. This meditation is about "catching our blessings," making sure we do not miss them and go around with an empty spot that could be filled with love.

In this meditation, the children decide where their blessings are needed and put them wherever they feel they need more love. This can be in their hearts, their minds, their hands, their feet, or even an elbow.

Creative Ideas

Materials

Meditation pillow—any pillow, folded blanket, rug; any spot you create inside or outside.

Indian rattle—baby rattle on a decorated stick; decorated stick with bells.

Terms

"Blessings"—love drops, gifts of love.

Uses

Use this meditation anytime a child needs love.

Use when a child feels a void or a loss and needs to fill it with love.

Use to teach a child how to accept love blessings.

Use to teach a child that we can all give blessings to one another.

Your Own Creative Ideas

Catching Blessings Meditation

This meditation teaches children that there are blessings within them and all around them, and that at every moment, we all have the power to give and receive these loving blessings.

Materials
- Meditation pillows
- Indian rattle

Arrange the meditation pillows in a circle with the Indian rattle in the center.

"We are going to sit with our legs crossed, our backs straight, and our heads held high. Our hands are in the begging bowl position.

Shake the Indian rattle over the children in a large circle in front of you and say:

"May this circle be surrounded in light and love."

State your intent, such as: "We are reaching out for the blessings all around us."

"Get ready to catch your blessings. Be thinking about where you need them. Maybe in your heart for loving feelings, in your throat for loving words, or in your mind for loving thoughts."

Shake the Indian rattle over each child's hands, which are reaching out in the begging bowl position. Have the children catch the blessings and put their hands where they feel they need love.

"Okay, is everyone all filled up, or are you ready for more?"

Shake the rattle over the outstretched hands of the children who feel they need more blessings. When you are finished giving blessings, shake the Indian rattle over the children in a large circle in front of you again and say the following mantra:

Mantra: "We are always blessed."

Inviting the Bell
Meditation

Lisa teaching the "Inviting the Bell Meditation" using the energy chime

Inviting the Bell
Meditation

"Lisa, I know what you are thinking.
You are thinking how much you love us."

—*Three-year-old Joseph*

Introduction

I created this meditation after a visit to a Buddhist retreat where I learned to listen to the bell.

Children love all kinds of sounds, and they love the sound of a bell. Teaching a child to stop and listen to a bell when rung, from the beginning to the very end of the sound, teaches him or her how to be still and quiet and to listen, on the inside and the outside—how to be in the moment.

When I introduce the bell to children, I say, "When I ring this bell, I am thinking how much I love you and how happy I am to be with you today."

The sound of the bell can be used to change an overactive, loud, or negative energy to a calm, peaceful, and loving energy. It can also be used as a gentle way to let children know that something important is about to be said or that an activity is about to change.

Creative Ideas

Materials

Meditation pillow—any pillow, folded blanket, rug; any spot you create inside or outside.

Single-tone bell—any metal bowl, bell, or singing bowl.

Striker—wooden spoon or dowel.

Terms

"Strike the bell"—ring the bell.

Uses

Use this meditation anytime a child needs focus, to be reminded to be in the moment.

Use anytime a child needs to be filled up with love, to be reminded he or she is loved.

Use anytime a child misses someone, to send the child's love.

Use anytime a child needs negative behavior changed to positive energy.

■

Your Own Creative Ideas

Inviting the Bell Meditation

This meditation teaches children how to be silent within themselves, how to honor and be in the moment.

Materials

- Meditation pillows
- Singing bowl
- Striker

Arrange the meditation pillows in a circle with the bell and striker in the center.

"We are going to sit with our legs crossed, our backs straight, and our heads held high. Our hands are in the begging bowl position and our eyes are looking at the bell in the center of the circle."

Strike the bell.

Listen until the bell quiets.

"May this circle be surrounded in light and love."

State your intent, such as: "To honor and be in this moment together."

"When I strike this bell, I am thinking about how much I love you—how happy I am to have you here with me. So when you hear the sound of this bell, it is the sound of my love for you."

Strike the bell.

Listen until the bell quiets.

"Now we are going to listen to the sound of the bell and wonder, 'Where is the sound of that bell going?'"

Strike the bell.

Sit quietly gazing up and around until the bell quiets.

"Let's send the sound of the bell with our love all around our home and to our whole family."

Strike the bell.

"There it goes. There goes our love all around our home and to our whole family. They are all getting filled with love."

Listen until the bell quiets.

"Now let's invite the sound of the bell to fill ourselves up with love."

Strike the bell.

"Here it comes. Breathe in the sound of the bell. We are all getting filled up with love."

Listen until the bell quiets.

Mantra: "We are all *full* of love today."

Walking Meditation

Lisa gathering the children in a circle

Walking Meditation

Introduction

$\mathcal{T}$aking the time to observe and be in nature with your child is a wonderful gift to give. Wondering aloud and asking questions like: "I wonder where that bird is going?" "Look at those leaves dance in the wind." "Feel that warm sunshine?" Give your child the time to wonder, observe, and learn about the natural world.

Children are very curious and have long attention spans when they are interested. "Nature" interests children.

This meditation can be used when out on walks in the city, driving in the car, looking out a window, sitting in a waiting room, or entering a new home or building.

Take the time to observe what's around your child. Let your child's eyes stay long enough on what he or she is watching. Comment on what the sounds are, where they are from, what people are doing, where people are going. Let your child's eyes linger as he or she watches a construction site, watches the mail carrier, watches the baker. Everything and everyone in life interests children. We need to take the time to acknowledge, honor, and allow this time.

Creative Ideas

Materials

Tibetan horn—any horn or instrument will do. Instead of saying the Om chant in this meditation, I blow my Tibetan horn three times and call all the animals, trees, and air to get ready, because the children are coming. The children love this! My horn sounds like an elephant to them.

Terms

"In a loving way"—true nature, with openness.

Uses

Use this meditation inside as well as outside, when visiting a new home, a museum, the ocean, a city, anywhere. Children are naturally curious about all of life; everyone and everything interests them.

I use this meditation when children are new to my home, to teach them about the things in my home that they can touch and the things that are just to be looked at. I tell them where I bought things or who gave them to me, what they mean to me. I show them what's behind each door, where and what each room is. I believe this knowledge helps children to be successful, to feel empowered and comfortable.

Your Own Creative Ideas

Walking Meditation

This joyful walk teaches children respect, honor, and responsibility for their environment.

Materials
- Tibetan horn (optional)

Gather the children in a circle outside.

Put one arm up and make a large circle in front of you over the children's heads and say: "Surround these children in light and love."

State your intent, such as: "To see, hear, and feel the loving joy in the world around us."

(*Touching your feet*)
"May these feet walk on the path of love."

(*Touching your hand*)
"May these hands touch in a loving way."

(*Touching your eyes*)
"May these eyes see in a loving way."

(*Touching your ears*)
"May these ears hear in a loving way."

(*Touching your nose*)
"May this nose smell in a loving way."

(*Touching your mouth*)
"May this mouth speak in a loving way."

(*Touching your forehead*)
"May this mind think in a loving way."

Together chant: "Ommm, Ommm, Ommm."

Or blow the Tibetan horn three times and say: "Calling all the birds, insects, animals, flowers, and trees, who all vibrate with love. Here we come on our walk."

Begin marching in rhythm to the following chant:

"Let—love—guide—us."

"Let—love—guide—us."

"Let—love—guide—us."

As you go on your walk look at, smell, and touch all the nature around you. Take the opportunity to stop, look, and listen.

Ask such questions as: "I wonder where that bird is going?" "I wonder how high that butterfly can fly?" "I wonder where that squirrel lives?" "How did that tree grow so tall?" Ask questions to broaden the children's minds, not to get answers. *It is all about the children being involved in the world around them.*

At the end of the walk, gather in a circle and take a moment to express your gratitude:

"We thank the trees for cleaning the air and keeping the birds safe. We are thankful to the rain for giving us water to drink and for giving the fish and frogs a place to live. We thank the sun for keeping us warm and for growing our food and flowers."

Stretch one arm out and make a large circle in front of you and say the following mantra:

Mantra: "We are grateful for the loving gifts of nature."

Gratitude
Meditation

Hannah—two years old

Gratitude Meditation

"I am grateful for my sister, Greer."

—*Three-year-old Walker*

Introduction

We have so much to be grateful for. I have seen the joy children feel when they express their gratitude.

This meditation is a chance for children not only to learn the importance of being grateful, but to learn to express their gratitude for what really matters in their lives: family, friends, community, home, and the world around them.

We can all find something each day to be grateful for.

Creative Ideas

Materials

Meditation pillow—any pillow, folded blanket, rug; any spot you create inside or outside.

Singing bowl—any metal bowl, bell, or single-tone energy chime.

Striker—wooden spoon or dowel.

Indian Rattle—baby rattle on a decorated stick; decorated stick with bells.

Terms

"Teacher"—parent, grandparent, or friend.

"To teach"—to parent, grandparent, to guide.

Uses

Use this meditation to teach gratefulness for what we receive.

Use to express gratitude for a child's birth.

Use on each birthday to express gratitude for a child's birth.

Use to express gratitude after receiving gifts on holidays and birthdays.

Use when family and friends visit, in gratitude for their time with us.

Use to teach gratefulness for our world, and all it gives us.

Use to teach gratefulness for family, friends, home, school.

Use at mealtime to teach gratefulness for our food and the people who made it.

Use to express gratitude for someone who has passed on or for an event that has ended.

Your Own Creative Ideas

Gratitude Meditation

This meditation teaches children the importance of taking time to be grateful for all of life's gifts.

Materials
- Meditation pillows
- Singing bowl
- Striker
- Indian rattle

Arrange the meditation pillows in a circle with the singing bowl, striker, and Indian rattle in the center.

"We are going to sit with our legs crossed, our backs straight, and our heads held high. Our hands are in the begging bowl position and our eyes are looking at the bowl in the center of the circle."

Strike the bowl.

Listen until the bowl quiets.

Shake the Indian rattle over the children in a large circle in front of you and say:

"May this circle be surrounded in light and love."

State your intent, such as: "To teach you the importance of taking the time to be grateful."

"I'm going to strike the bowl and we will breathe three times. The first breath we will breathe in will be love."

Strike the bowl.

"Breathe in love."
(Long exaggerated breath in)

"Breathe out sadness."
(Long exaggerated breath out)

Strike the bowl.

"Breathe in joy."
(Long exaggerated breath in)

"Breathe out madness."
(Long exaggerated breath out)

Strike the bowl.

"Breathe in peace."
(Long exaggerated breath in)

"Breathe out badness."
(Long exaggerated breath out)

"All of my sadness, madness, and badness changes to bright white sparkles of love."

"I am so grateful to have you here today. Thank you for being with me."

Strike the bowl.

Place your hands crossed over your heart chakra. Stretch your hands out in gratitude to the first child on your right and say:

"Ommm, Ommm, Ommm, I am so grateful to [child's name] for being here today."

Repeat for each child.

Now, starting with the child on your right, say:

"[Child's name], what do you feel grateful for today?"

When the child has answered, have all the children place their hands crossed over their heart chakras.

Strike the bowl.

Raise your arms and eyes to the sky while you chant the following:

"Ommm, Ommm, Ommm, [child's name] is grateful for . . ."

Repeat for each child.

"Now we will end the meditation with three cleansing breaths of love."

Strike the bowl.

"Breathe in love."
(Long exaggerated breath in)

"Breathe out sadness."
(Long exaggerated breath out)

Strike the bowl.

"Breathe in joy."
(Long exaggerated breath in)

"Breathe out madness."
(Long exaggerated breath out)

Strike the bowl.

"Breathe in peace."
(Long exaggerated breath in)

"Breathe out badness."
(Long exaggerated breath out)

"All of my sadness, madness, and badness changes to bright white sparkles of love."

Pick up the Indian rattle and say:

"Put your hands in the begging bowl position and get ready to catch your blessings."

Shake the Indian rattle over each child's hands so the child may catch his or her blessings.

"Put your blessings where you need them—in your heart for loving feelings, in your mind for loving thoughts, in your throat for loving words."

When all the children are finished filling themselves with blessings, shake the Indian rattle in a large circle in front of you and say the following mantra:

Mantra: "We are so grateful for all we have."

Singing Bowl Meditation

Nicole teaching her three-year-old daughter, Sophia, about vibration

Singing Bowl Meditation

"Help, I need a singing bowl!
George has gone through every bowl in the house and said,
'No, that's not it, Mom.'"

— *Mother of three-year-old George*

Introduction

This is a favorite of the children, and I am asked frequently to make the bowl "sing" on their hands so they can hear and feel their love vibration.

I balance the bowl on the child's flat palm while holding his or her hand in mine and say, "Let's find your love vibration." Then when I circle the rim of the metal bowl with a wooden striker, the bowl begins to vibrate and "sing." "There it is. That is what your love vibration sounds and feels like. All things vibrate love."

Children love how the vibration tickles their palms.

Creative Ideas

Materials

Meditation pillow—any pillow, folded blanket, rug; any spot you create inside or outside.

Singing bowl—any metal bowl.

Striker—wooden spoon or dowel.

Indian rattle—baby rattle on a decorated stick; decorated stick with bells.

Terms

"Love vibration"—energy.

"Tickle"—vibrate.

Uses

Use this meditation to teach children about the vibration and energy that everyone and everything has. I teach that music, words, and every action we make move energy and create a vibration. We can all vibrate love for ourselves, others, and the world around us.

Your Own Creative Ideas

Singing Bowl Meditation

This meditation teaches children about vibration, that everything has vibration and everything vibrates love.

Materials

- Meditation pillows
- Singing bowl
- Striker
- Indian rattle

Arrange the meditation pillows in a circle with the singing bowl, striker, and Indian rattle in the center.

"We are going to sit with our legs crossed, our backs straight, and our heads held high. Our hands are in the begging bowl position and our eyes are looking at the bowl in the center of the circle."

Strike the bowl.

Listen until the bowl quiets.

Shake the Indian rattle over the children in a large circle in front of you and say:

"May this circle be surrounded in light and love."

State your intent, such as: "To teach you that everything has a love vibration."

"I'm going to strike the bowl and we will breathe three times. The first breath we will breathe in will be love."

Strike the bowl.

"Breathe in love."
(Long exaggerated breath in)

"Breathe out sadness."
(Long exaggerated breath out)

Strike the bowl.

"Breathe in joy."
(Long exaggerated breath in)

"Breathe out madness."
(Long exaggerated breath out)

Strike the bowl.

"Breathe in peace."
(Long exaggerated breath in)

"Breathe out badness."
(Long exaggerated breath out)

"All the sadness, madness, and badness changes to bright white sparkles of love."

"Now we are going to hear what my love vibration sounds like."

Balance the singing bowl on your palm and circle the outside rim with the wooden striker until the bowl "sings."

"Can you hear that? That is the sound of my love vibration. It tickles. Everything and everyone has a love vibration."

"Let's go around the circle so you can all feel and hear your own love vibration."

■

While holding each child's hand in yours, balance the singing bowl on the child's palm and circle the outside rim with the wooden striker until the bowl "sings."

"Can you feel that tickle? That is your love vibration. Can you hear that? That is what your love sounds like."

When you have finished finding each child's love vibration, place the singing bowl in the center of the circle and say:

"Now we will end our meditation with three cleansing breaths of love."

Strike the bowl.

"Breathe in love."
(Long exaggerated breath in)

"Breathe out sadness."
(Long exaggerated breath out)

Strike the bowl.

"Breathe in joy."
(Long exaggerated breath in)

"Breathe out madness."
(Long exaggerated breath out)

■

Strike the bowl.

"Breathe in peace."
(Long exaggerated breath in)

"Breathe out badness."
(Long exaggerated breath out)

"All the sadness, madness, and badness changes to bright white sparkles of love."

Pick up the Indian rattle and say:

"Put your hands in the begging bowl position and get ready to catch your blessings."

Shake the Indian rattle over each child's hands so the child may catch his or her blessings.

"Put your blessings where you need them—in your heart for loving feelings, in your throat for loving words, or in your mind for loving thoughts."

When all the children are finished filling themselves with blessings, shake the Indian rattle over the children in a large circle in front of you and say the following mantra:

Mantra: "Everything vibrates love."

Crystal Meditation

Sophie, two years old, opening her throat
so that her loving words can come out

Crystal Meditation

"I think my love got stuck!"

—*Three-year-old Wyatt*

Introduction

We all have love inside of us.

We can all make the choice to spend our days speaking, thinking, touching, and listening in a kind and loving way.

It is important that children understand that these loving feelings are already within them; the crystal just helps to open the way if and when their loving feelings get "stuck."

Creative Ideas

Materials

Meditation pillow—any pillow, folded blanket, rug; any spot you create inside or outside.

Singing bowl—any metal bowl, bell, or single-tone energy chime.

Striker—wooden spoon or dowel.

Indian rattle—baby rattle on a decorated stick; decorated stick with bells.

Rose quartz crystal—pinecone, stone, flower, anything that feels special to you or your child.

Terms

"Opening up my throat for loving words/my hands for my loving touch."

"Using my feet to walk in a loving way."

"My eyes to see in a loving way."

Uses

Use this meditation at the beginning of the day or an event.

Use to teach a child who has hit to open his or her hands for loving touch.

Use to teach a child who is overactive to use his or her feet to walk in a loving way.

Use to teach a child who has spoken unkindly to open his or her throat for loving words.

I hand the crystal to a child if the child's love gets "stuck" during the day, and the child holds it until he or she is "unstuck."

Your Own Creative Ideas

Crystal Meditation

This meditation teaches children that they are responsible for themselves—what they say, how they touch, what they think—and that they have the choice to live life in a kind and loving way.

Materials

- Meditation pillows
- Singing bowl
- Striker
- Indian rattle
- Rose quartz crystal

■

Arrange the meditation pillows in a circle with the singing bowl, striker, Indian rattle, and rose quartz in the center.

"We are going to sit with our legs crossed, our backs straight, and our heads held high. Our hands are in the begging bowl position and our eyes are looking at the bowl in the center of the circle."

Strike the bowl.

Listen until the bowl quiets.

Shake the Indian rattle over the children in a large circle in front of you and say:

"May this circle be surrounded in light and love."

State your intent, such as: "We can all choose to touch, speak, and think in a loving way."

"I'm going to strike the bowl and we will breathe three times. The first breath we will breathe in will be love."

Strike the bowl.

"Breathe in love."
(Long exaggerated breath in)

∎

"Breathe out sadness."
(Long exaggerated breath out)

Strike the bowl.

"Breathe in joy."
(Long exaggerated breath in)

"Breathe out madness."
(Long exaggerated breath out)

Strike the bowl.

"Breathe in peace."
(Long exaggerated breath in)

"Breathe out badness."
(Long exaggerated breath out)

"All the sadness, madness, and badness changes to bright white sparkles of love."

Strike the bowl.

Hold the crystal in both hands over your heart chakra as you rock back and forth.

"I am opening up my heart for my loving feelings, Ommm, Ommm, Ommm."

Move the crystal to your throat with both hands.

"I am opening up my throat for my loving words, Ommm, Ommm, Ommm."

Move the crystal to your forehead with both hands.

"I am opening up my mind for loving thoughts, Ommm, Ommm, Ommm."

Offer the crystal with both hands to the first child on your right.

Strike the bowl.

(Rocking back and forth)
"[Child's name] is opening up his heart for his loving feelings, Ommm, Ommm, Ommm."

Child moves the crystal to his throat chakra.

"[Child's name] is opening up his throat for his loving words, Ommm, Ommm, Ommm."

Child moves crystal to his forehead.

"[Child's name] is opening up his mind for his loving thoughts, Ommm, Ommm, Ommm."

He passes the crystal to the child on his right. Continue with the same striking of the bell and the three chants until all the children are done.

Put your cupped hands out and have the last child place the crystal in your hands. Place the crystal in the center of the circle.

"Now we will end the meditation with three cleansing breaths of love."

Strike the bowl.

"Breathe in love."
(Long exaggerated breath in)

"Breathe out sadness."
(Long exaggerated breath out)

Strike the bowl.

"Breathe in joy."
(Long exaggerated breath in)

"Breathe out madness."
(Long exaggerated breath out)

Strike the bowl.

"Breathe in peace."
(Long exaggerated breath in)

"Breathe out badness."
(Long exaggerated breath out)

"All the sadness, madness, and badness changes to bright white sparkles of love."

Pick up the Indian rattle and say:

"Put your hands in the begging bowl position and get ready to catch your blessings."

Shake the Indian rattle over each child's hands so the child may catch his or her blessings.

"Put your blessings where you need them—in your heart for loving feelings, in your throat for loving words, or in your mind for loving thoughts."

When all the children are finished filling themselves with blessings, shake the Indian rattle over the children in a large circle in front of you and say the following mantra:

Mantra: "We are all *opened up* with love."

Rainbow
Meditation

Walker, three years old, and his mom,
Cheryl, sending a healing rainbow of love

Rainbow Meditation

"Lisa, my grandpa sent me a rainbow!"

—*A happy three-year-old*

Introduction

This child loved his grandpa, and when his grandpa died unexpectedly, his sadness was palpable. In our meditation that day, we sent his grandpa a "healing rainbow of love," because we knew that his grandpa was sad, too—he missed his grandson and he didn't get to say good-bye. I told the child that whenever he needed to send love to his grandpa, he could send him a "healing rainbow of love." The following week when he visited his grandpa's grave, the child looked up and saw a double rainbow.

We all have a "healing rainbow of love" inside of us. It is ours to heal ourselves as well as ours to send anywhere to anyone who needs it.

■

Creative Ideas

Materials

Meditation pillow—any pillow, folded blanket, rug; any spot you create inside or outside.

Singing bowl—any metal bowl, bell, or single-tone energy chime.

Striker—wooden spoon or dowel.

Indian rattle—baby rattle on a decorated stick; decorated stick with bells.

Terms

Chakra—one of the seven energy centers of the body with its corresponding color.

Uses

Use this meditation to send a rainbow of love to anyone or anything that you or your child feels needs it—family members, the earth. . . .

Use to send a rainbow of love to family members who have died.

Use to send a rainbow of love to pets who have died.

Use to send a rainbow of love to people and places when sad events happen and more love is needed.

Your Own Creative Ideas

Rainbow Meditation

This meditation teaches children that love can be sent and received. It gives children the opportunity to heal themselves and others.

Materials
- Meditation pillows
- Singing bowl
- Striker
- Indian rattle

Arrange the meditation pillows in a circle with the singing bowl, striker, and Indian rattle in the center.

"We are going to sit with our legs crossed, our backs straight, and our heads held high. Our hands are in the begging bowl position and our eyes are looking at the bowl in the center of the circle."

Strike the bowl.

Listen until the bowl quiets.

Shake the Indian rattle over the children in a large circle in front of you and say:

"May this circle be surrounded in light and love."

State your intent, such as: "We can send healing love within ourselves to others and the world around us."

"I'm going to strike the bowl and we will breathe three times. The first breath we will breathe in will be love."

Strike the bowl.

"Breathe in love."
(Long exaggerated breath in)

"Breathe out sadness."
(Long exaggerated breath out)

■

Strike the bowl.

"Breathe in joy."
(Long exaggerated breath in)

"Breathe out madness."
(Long exaggerated breath out)

Strike the bowl.

"Breathe in peace."
(Long exaggerated breath in)

"Breathe out badness."
(Long exaggerated breath out)

"All the sadness, madness, and badness changes to bright white sparkles of love."

"Now we are going to send our healing rainbows up and out the tops of our heads. Here we go. . . ."

As your right hand rises up from the begging bowl position to the top of your head, say:

"Red" *(begging bowl position)*

■

"Orange" *(below belly button)*

"Yellow" *(above belly button)*

"Green" *(heart chakra)*

"Blue" *(throat chakra)*

"Indigo" *(forehead, third eye)*

"Violet" *(top of your head)*

Wave your hand over the children in a large circle in front of you and say:

"Now we are making a big circle rainbow around us. Now let's spin the rainbow circle so that we are inside a rainbow ball. Okay, here we are inside the rainbow ball of love."

"Now give the rainbow ball anything sad, mad, or bad that you don't want, and the rainbow will change it into love."

Give the rainbow what you do not want, gesturing with your hands. You or the children may choose to vocalize this or not.

"The rainbow ball is all full of healing love. Let's take what we need from the rainbow and fill ourselves up with healing love."

Reach up into the air and grab the pieces of the rainbow that you need and place them in your heart chakra.

"Now we are going to send the rainbow to our whole town, there it goes, out the window all over and around our town now, tell all the children to give the rainbow what is sad, mad, or bad, and the rainbow will change it to love."

"Children of our town, give the rainbow all of your sadness, madness, and badness, and it will change it into love."

"Now let's tell the children of our town to take what they need from the rainbow and fill themselves up with love."

"Children of our town, take what you need from the rainbow and fill yourselves up with love."

"Now let's take that rainbow ball and spin it around all the children in America."

"Tell the children of America to give the rainbow anything that makes them sad, mad, or bad, and the rainbow will change it into love."

"Children of America, give the rainbow all of your sadness, madness, and badness, and it will change into love."

"Now let's tell the children of America to take what they need from the rainbow and fill themselves up with love."

"Children of America, take what you need from the rainbow and fill yourselves up with love."

"Now let's send the rainbow around the whole world and tell all the children of the world to give the rainbow all of their sadness, madness, and badness and that the rainbow will change it into love."

"Children of the world, give the rainbow all of your sadness, madness, and badness, and it will change it into love."

"Now let's tell the children of the world to take what they need from the rainbow and fill themselves up with love."

"Children of the world, take what you need from the rainbow and fill yourselves up with love."

"Now let's bring the healing rainbow ball of love back around us."

Wave your hand over the children in a large circle and say:

"Give anything you have left to the rainbow that makes you feel sad, mad, or bad, and it will be changed into love."

■

"Now we will bring our rainbow of love back inside of us."

Starting with your right hand at the top of your head and moving slowly down to the begging bowl position, say:

"Violet" *(top of your head)*

"Indigo" *(forehead, third eye)*

"Blue" *(throat chakra)*

"Green" *(heart chakra)*

"Yellow" *(above belly button)*

"Orange" *(below belly button)*

"Red" *(begging bowl position)*

"Now we will end the meditation with three cleansing breaths of love."

Strike the bowl.

"Breathe in love."
(Long exaggerated breath in)

■

"Breathe out sadness."
(Long exaggerated breath out)

Strike the bowl.

"Breathe in joy."
(Long exaggerated breath in)

"Breathe out madness."
(Long exaggerated breath out)

Strike the bowl.

"Breathe in peace."
(Long exaggerated breath in)

"Breathe out badness."
(Long exaggerated breath out)

"All the sadness, madness, and badness changes to bright white sparkles of love."

Pick up the Indian rattle and say:

"Put your hands in the begging bowl position and get ready to catch your blessings."

Shake the Indian rattle over each child's hands so the child may catch his or her blessings.

"Put your blessings where you need them—in your heart for loving feelings, in your throat for loving words, or in your mind for loving thoughts."

When all the children are finished filling themselves with blessings, shake the Indian rattle over the children in a large circle in front of you and say the following mantra:

Mantra: "Our world is surrounded in a healing rainbow ball of love."

In Closing

"Namaste"—Jackson, two years old

In Closing

At the beginning and end of this book, children are in the greeting position of *"Namaste."* *"Namaste"* means "From my jewel within me, my place of love, to your jewel within you, your place of love."

"Namaste" to each and every one of you.

—*Lisa*

Sending love to the children of the world

About the Author

Lisa lives, teaches, and writes in New England and has two grown children. She has developed a method of teaching meditation to children from eighteen months to three years old. She has been teaching this method since the mid-'90s. She has taught and volunteered with children from preschool to eighth grade since 1977 at schools in Maine, Georgia, California, and Vermont. From 1999 to 2002 she developed and taught a program for kindergarten through sixth grades on spirituality and meditation at All Souls Interfaith Gathering, a spiritual center in Vermont.

With a grant from the Brimmer Fund of Boston, Lisa traveled to Nepal and Tibet, where she studied meditation with Tibetan Monks and Hindu and Tibetan Buddhist scholars and guides. Lisa has met with and taught her meditations to doctors and nurses in the pediatric intensive care unit at the at the Floating Hospital for Children at Tufts–New England Medical Center in Boston, Massachusetts.

Lisa continues to teach meditation to preschool children. She also gives workshops on teaching and parenting to the spirit of a child.